This Book Belongs to

_____

Thank you for being our valued customer. We are so grateful for the pleasure of serving you and hope we met your expectations.

Learn To Write

Trace the words below and write your own.

S

Scoreboard

S is for Scoreboard

S is for Scoreboard

Puzzle Game

Write the letters in the box according to the lines.

H	E	T	M	E	L

Find the Path

Help the player to find his skates

Learn To Write

Trace the words below and write your own.

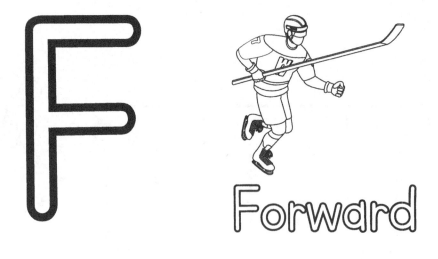

F

Forward

F is for Forward

F is for Forward

Puzzle Game

Write the letters in the box according to the lines.

T I K C S

Find the Path

Help the puck find the net

Learn To Write

Trace the words below and write your own.

Hockey Protection

H is for Hockey Protection

H is for Hockey Protection

Puzzle Game

Write the letters in the box according to the lines.

Find the Path

Help the player find their safety gear.

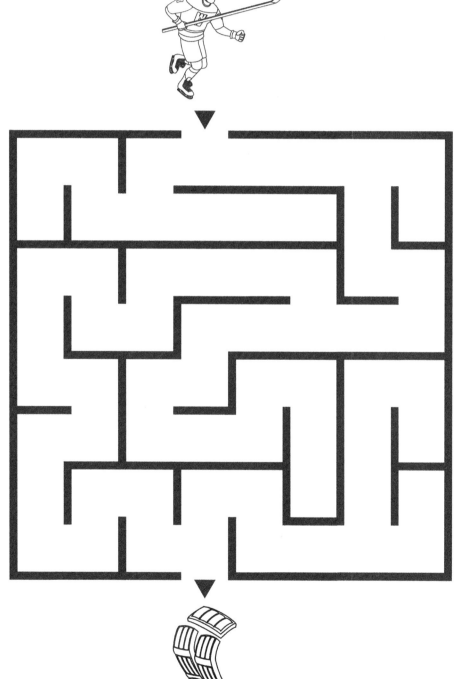

Learn To Write

Trace the words below and write your own.

N

Net

N is for Net

N is for Net

Find the Path

Help the players to find their hockey rink.

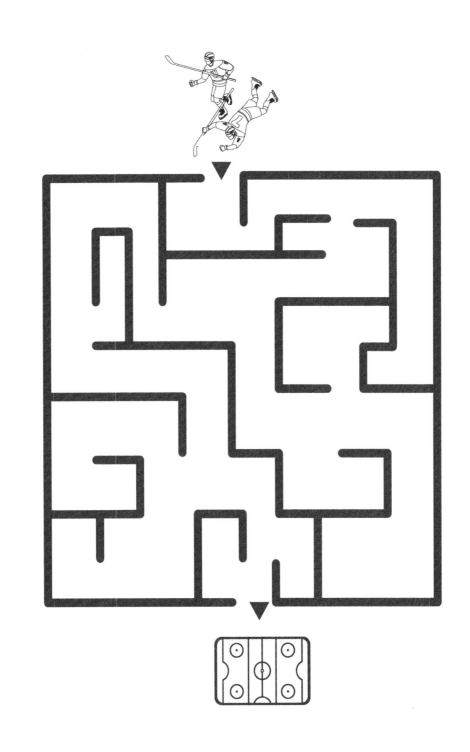

Writing Hockey

Look at the pictures. Trace the name of each picture.

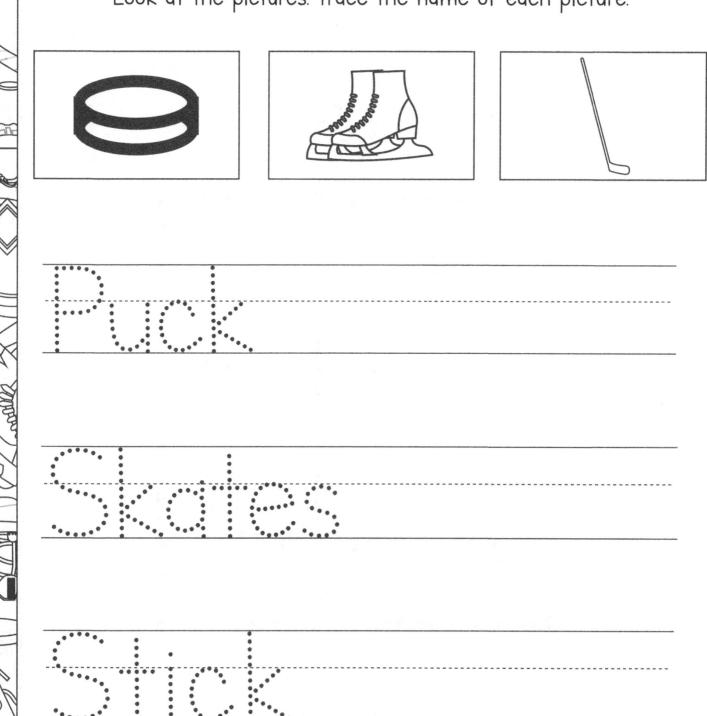

Puck

Skates

Stick

Find the Path

Help the referee find the whistle.

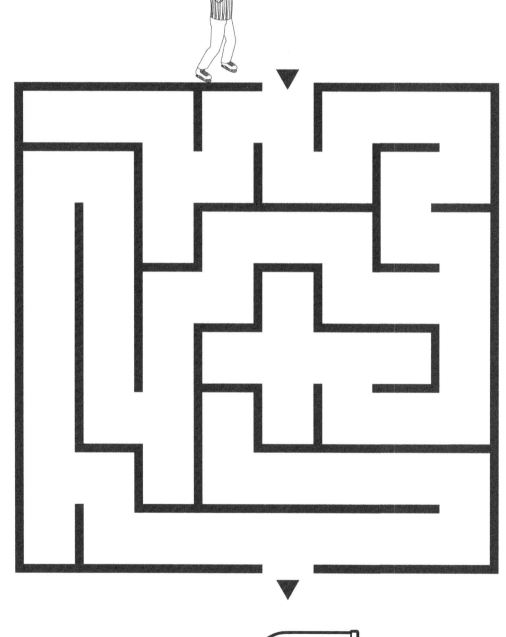

Word Search Puzzle

Find and circle the words in the puzzle.

P	U	C	K	W	V	F	H	G
A	Q	R	L	Y	J	D	R	O
S	T	I	C	K	Y	O	Q	A
W	X	Z	A	G	C	B	Z	L
J	B	Y	P	D	U	X	B	A
Z	A	M	B	O	N	I	F	R
R	H	W	D	L	Q	X	J	Z
F	A	C	E	O	F	F	V	Y

STICK   PUCK   FACEOFF
ZAMBONI   GOAL

Hockey Crossword Puzzle

Complete the Ice Hockey crossword
according to the words provided below

1. JERSEY   2. RINK   3. GLOVES

4. NET   5. HELMET

Missing Letters

Write the missing letters between A-Z.

	b	c	
d	___	f	
g	___	i	tr_phy

	k		m	n	___
p	q	r	___	t	u
___	w	___	y	___	

a	e	h	j	l
o	s	v	x	z

Word Search Puzzle

Find and circle the words in the puzzle.

C	F	O	P	Q	U	T	S	R
H	T	V	Z	G	O	L	Y	Q
E	P	R	E	F	E	N	S	E
C	W	I	S	Z	U	W	K	O
K	X	N	Q	N	E	T	Q	V
I	S	K	Y	Y	W	Z	P	W
N	O	L	S	X	Q	V	O	F
G	O	V	E	R	T	I	M	E

CHECKING RINK NET
OVERTIME GOL

Hockey Crossword Puzzle

Complete the Ice Hockey crossword
according to the words provided below

1. WHISTLE   2. STICK   3. CUP

4. PADS   5. SKATES

Missing Letters

Write the missing letters between A-Z.

a	___	c		
d	e	___	he_me_	
___	h	i		
j	___		m	___	o
___	q	r	___	t	u
v	w	___	y	___

b	f	g	k	l
n	p	s	x	z

Word Search Puzzle

Find and circle the words in the puzzle.

A	S	C	O	R	E	G	O	L
P	L	C	D	A	D	J	P	Y
E	A	G	Y	M	O	K	E	I
N	P	A	K	D	F	B	R	G
A	S	H	I	C	E	H	A	J
L	H	O	B	D	N	K	N	B
T	O	L	A	P	S	H	D	T
Y	T	B	H	Y	G	D	K	J

PENALTY   ICE

SLAPSHOT   SCORE

Puzzle Hockey

Cut out the pieces and stick them in the right places on the puzzle.

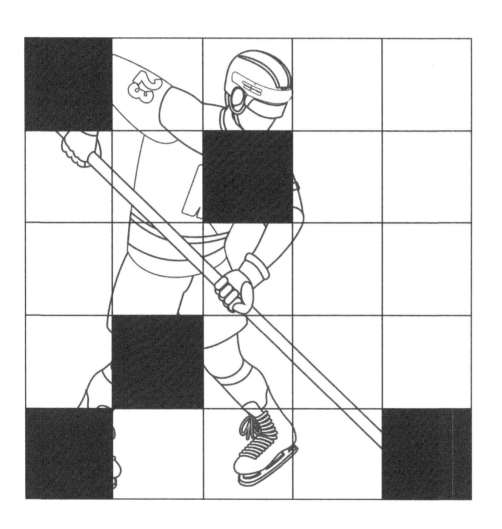
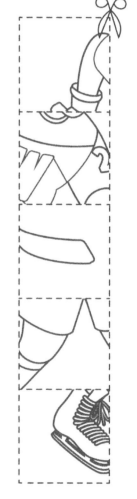

This page intentionally left blank

Match Puzzle Hockey

Cut out the pieces and stick them in the right places on the puzzle.

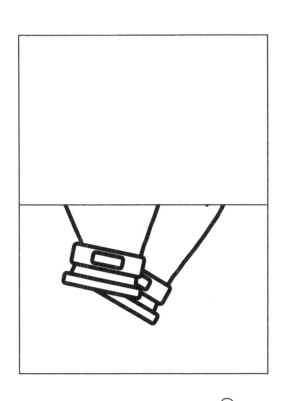

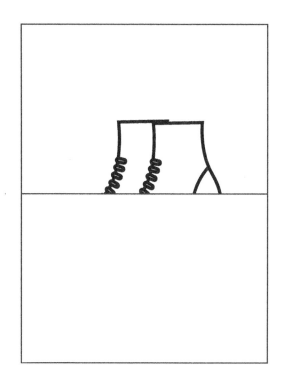

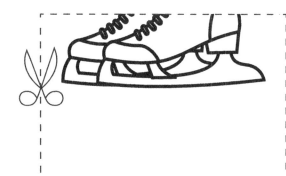

This page intentionally left blank

Puzzle Hockey

Cut out the pieces and stick them in the right places on the puzzle.

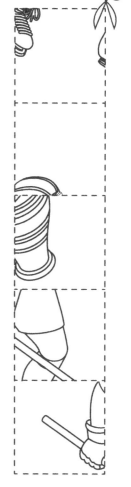

This page intentionally left blank

Match Puzzle Hockey

Cut out the pieces and stick them in the right places on the puzzle.

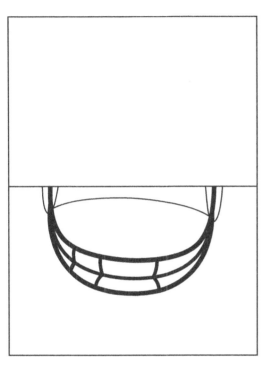

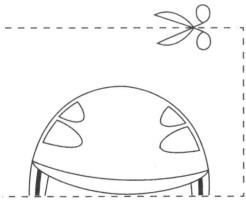
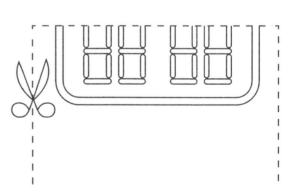

This page intentionally left blank

Puzzle Hockey

Cut out the pieces and stick them in the right places on the puzzle.

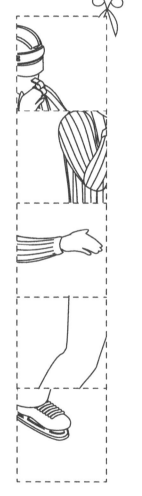

This page intentionally left blank

Missing Numbers

Write the missing numbers between 1-15.

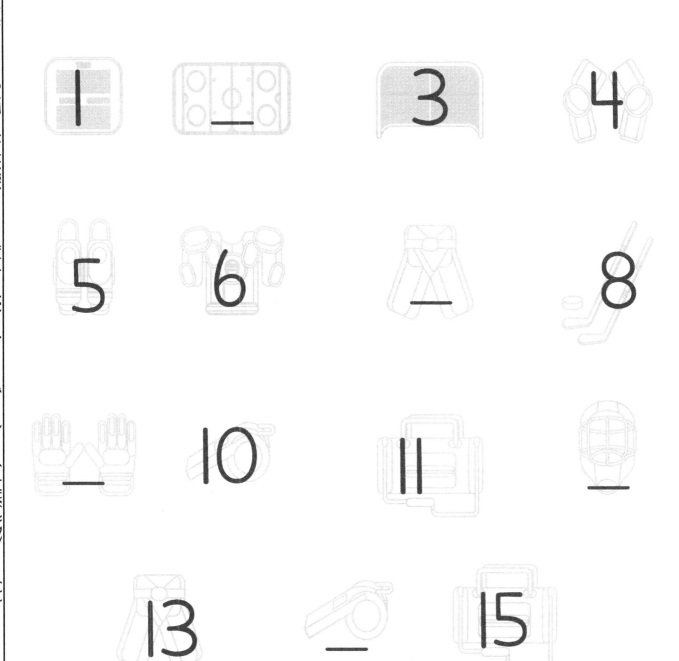

1   _   3   4

5   6   _   8

_   10   11   _

13   _   15

I Spy Hockey

How many of each of the items can you spy?

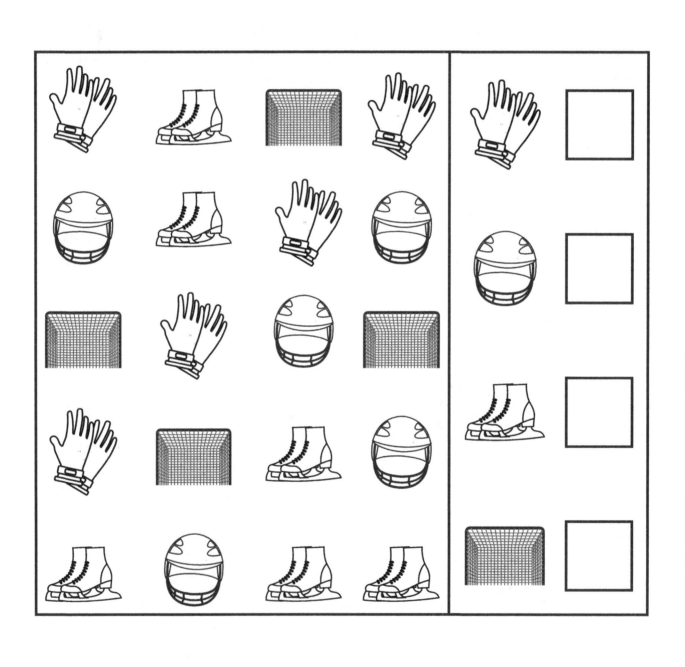

Big And Small

Look at the pictures in the boxes. Answer the questions
by circling the correct picture.

Which is bigger?

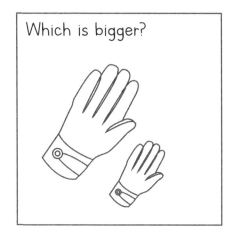

Which is smaller?

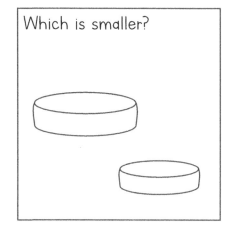

Which is smaller?

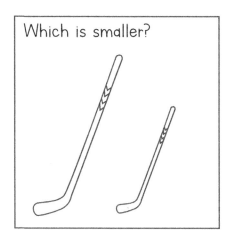

Which is bigger?

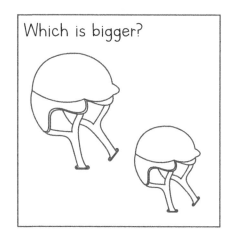

Which is bigger?

Which is smaller?

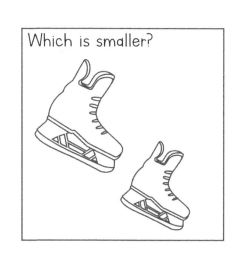

Missing Numbers

Write the missing numbers between 4-15.

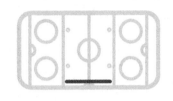 ___    5    ___

 7    ___    9

 10   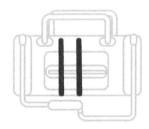 11    ___

 ___    14    15

I Spy Hockey

How many of each of the items can you spy?

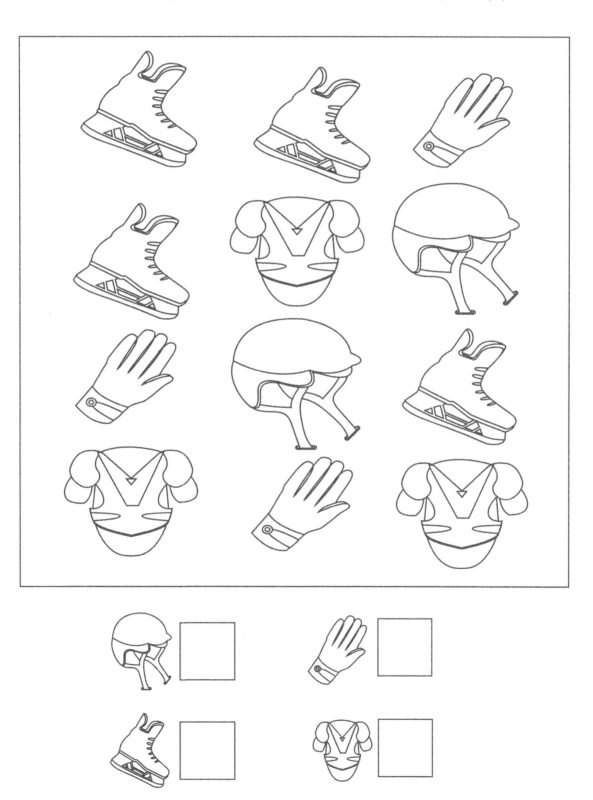

Big And Small

Look at the pictures in the boxes. Answer the questions by circling the correct picture.

Which is smaller?

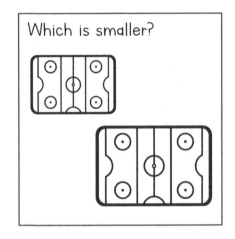

Which is bigger?

Which is bigger?

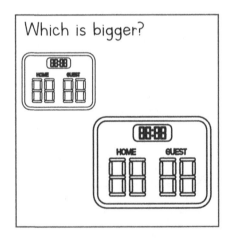

Which is smaller?

Which is smaller?

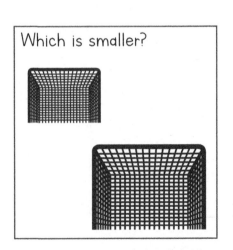

Which is bigger?

Missing Numbers

Write the missing numbers between 6-27.

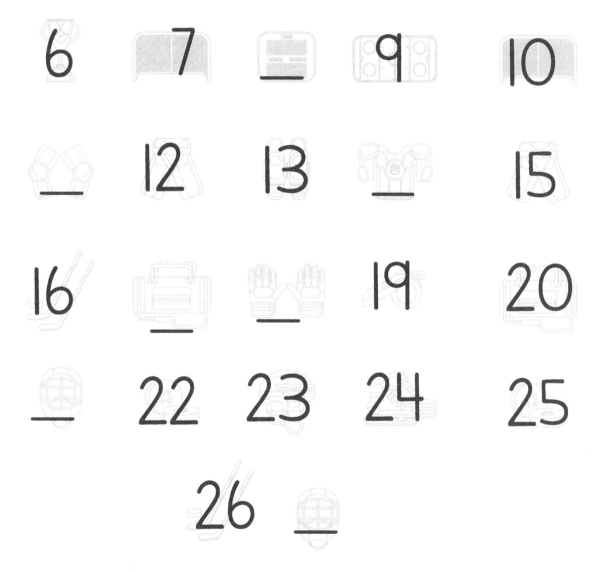

6   7   __   9   10

__   12   13   __   15

16   __   __   19   20

__   22   23   24   25

26   __

I Spy Hockey

How many of each of the items can you spy?

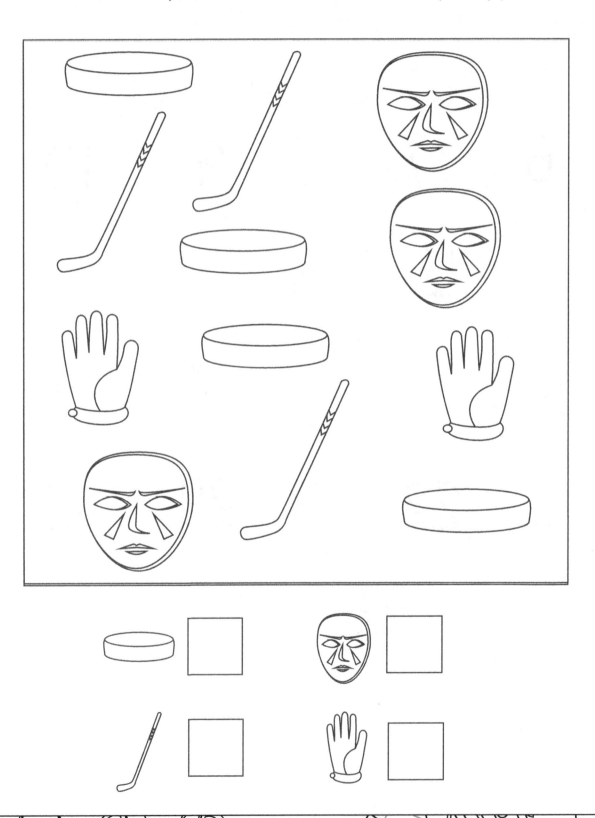

Big And Small

Look at the pictures in the boxes. Answer the questions
by circling the correct picture.

Which is bigger?

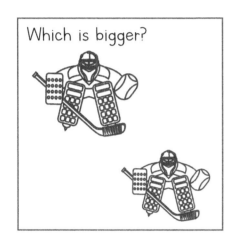

Which is smaller?

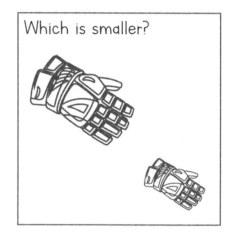

Which is smaller?

Which is bigger?

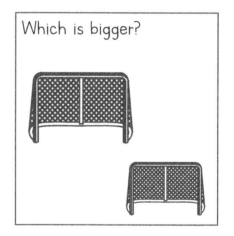

Which is bigger?

Which is smaller?

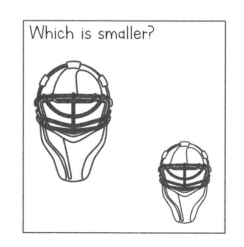

I Spy Hockey

How many of each of the items can you spy?

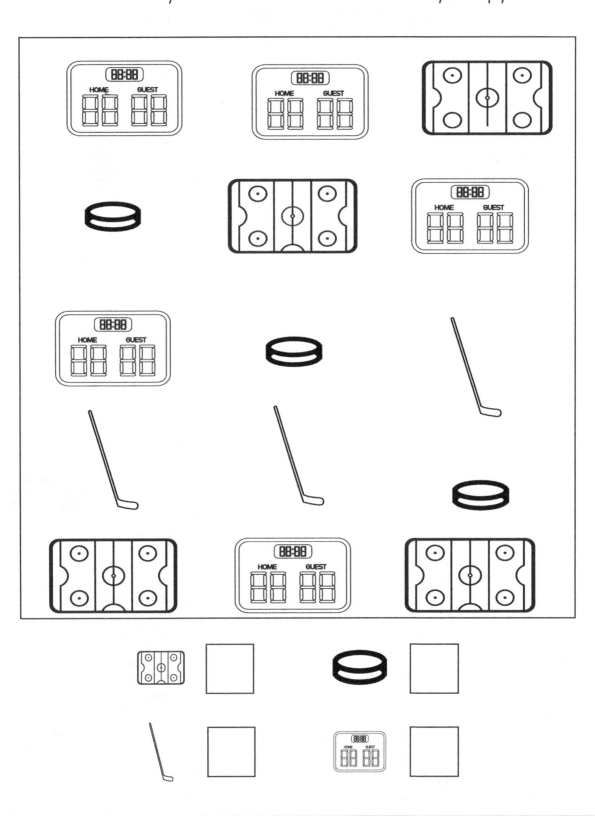

Big And Small

Look at the pictures in the boxes. Answer the questions by circling the correct picture.

Which is bigger?

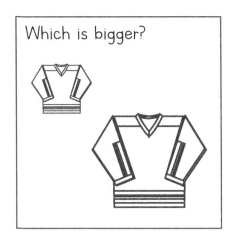

Which is smaller?

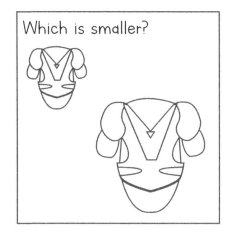

Which is smaller?

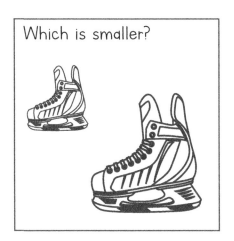

Which is bigger?

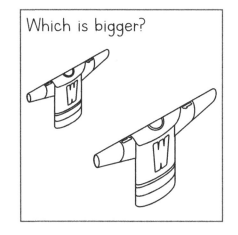

Which is bigger?

Which is smaller?

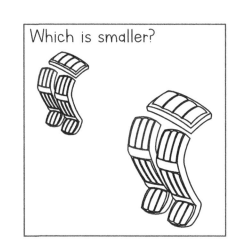

I Spy Hockey

How many of each of the items can you spy?

Big And Small

Look at the pictures in the boxes. Answer the questions by circling the correct picture.

Which is bigger?

Which is smaller?

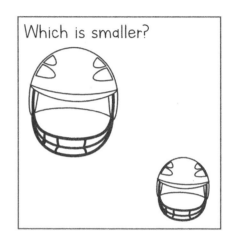

Which is smaller?

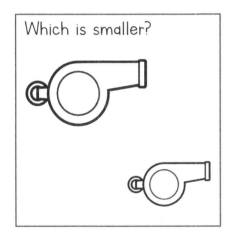

Which is bigger?

Which is bigger?

Which is smaller?

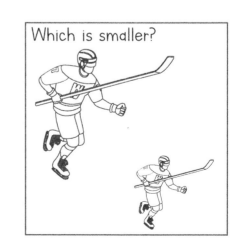

Another Size Order

Sort the images below from smallest to largest.

Introducing Hockey

Study the pictures below to get to know the sport of hockey.

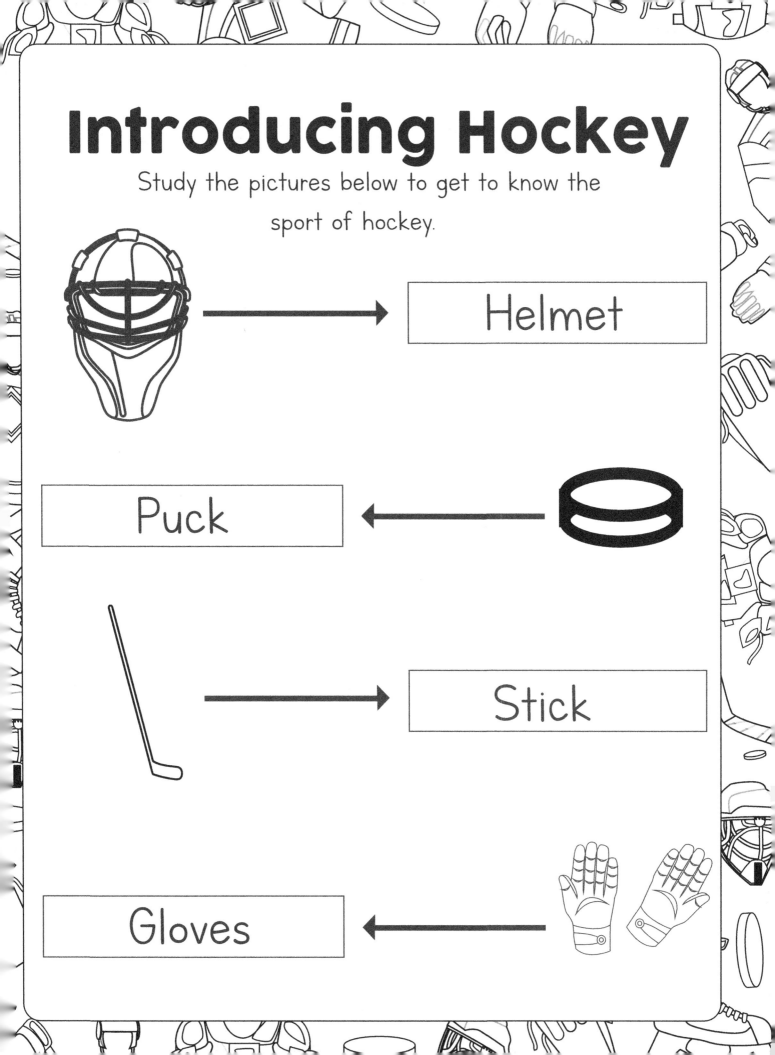

Helmet

Puck

Stick

Gloves

Introducing Hockey

Study the pictures below to get to know the sport of hockey.

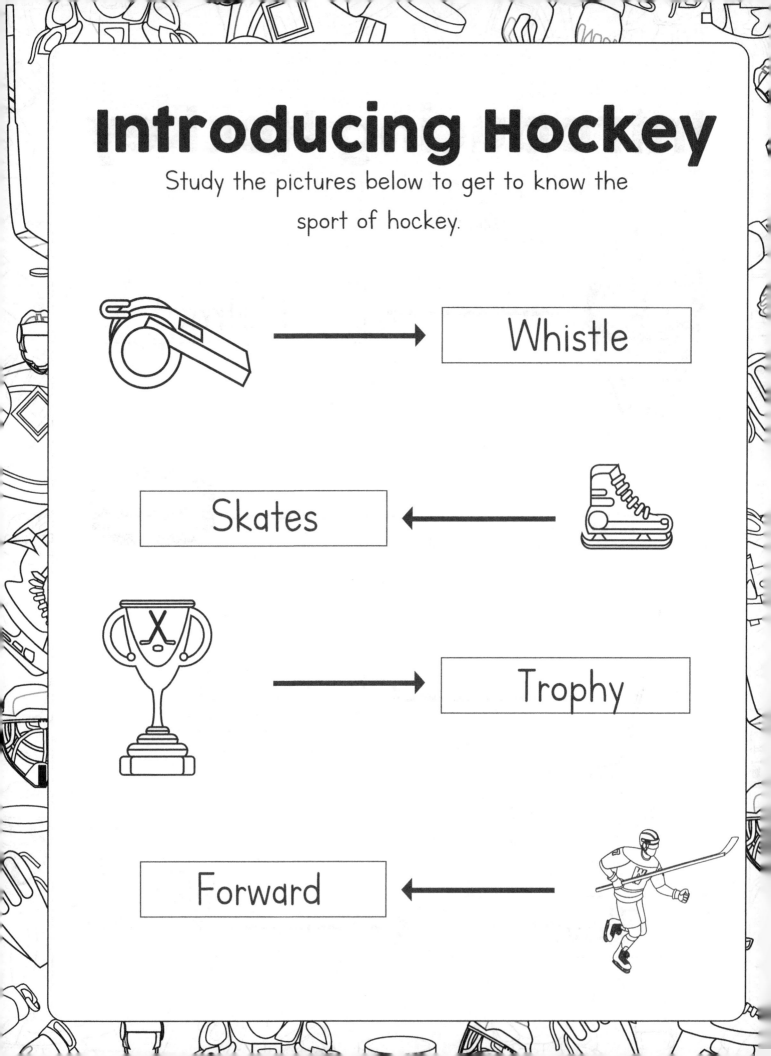

Whistle

Skates

Trophy

Forward

Introducing Hockey

Study the pictures below to get to know the sport of hockey.

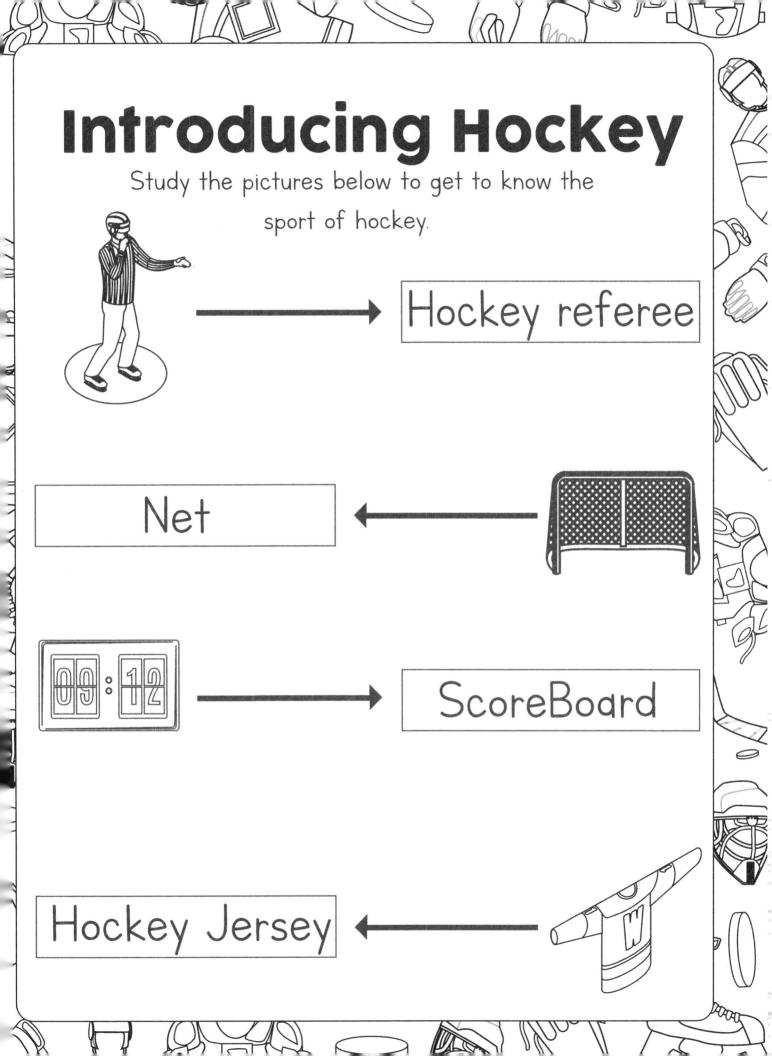

Hockey referee

Net

ScoreBoard

Hockey Jersey

Hockey Sport

Fill in the first letter of each word.

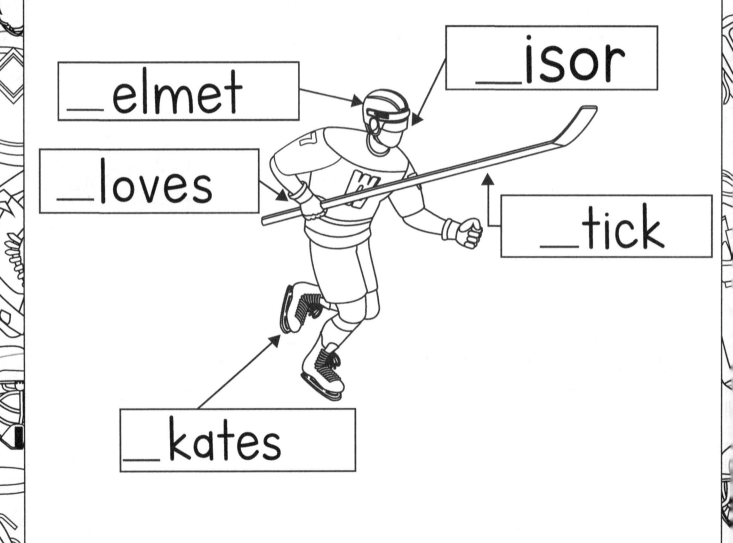

__isor

__elmet

__loves

__tick

__kates

Missing Letters

Complete the blanks below.

H S P G   N T S J

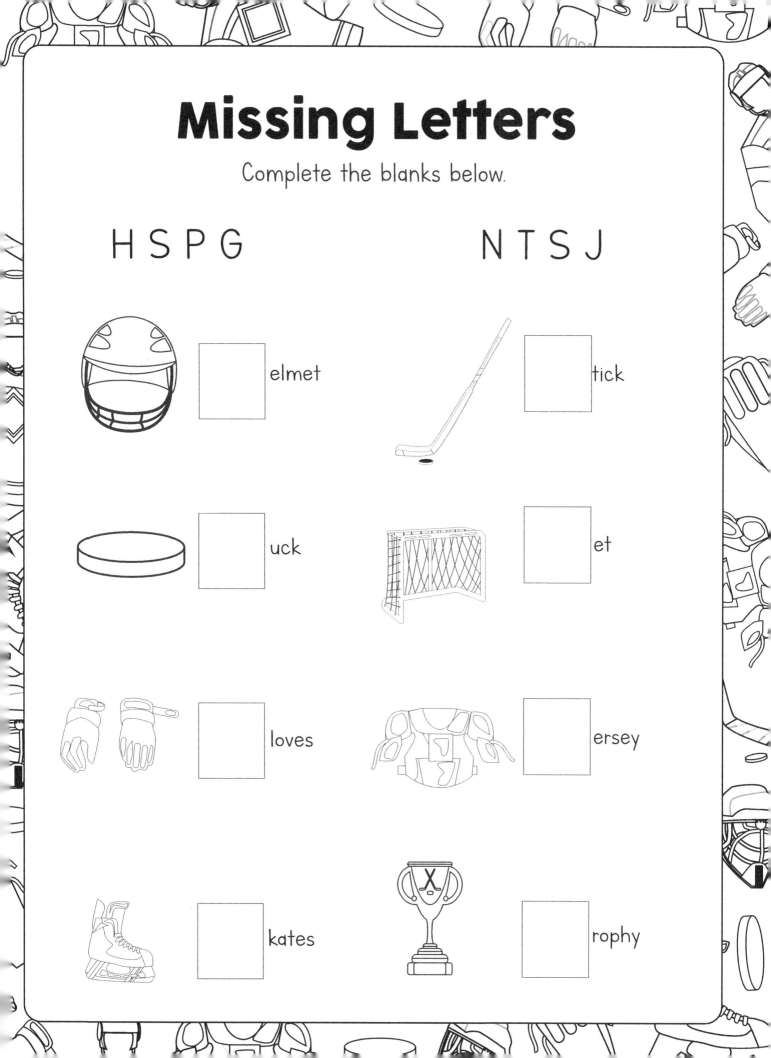

[ ] elmet

[ ] tick

[ ] uck

[ ] et

[ ] loves

[ ] ersey

[ ] kates

[ ] rophy

Missing Letters

Fill in the missing letter.

 ☐ ET

 ☐ ELMET

 ☐ ERSEY

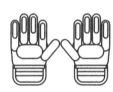 ☐ LOVES

 ☐ ROPHY

 ☐ TICK

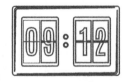 ☐ COREBOARD

 ☐ KATES

Which Is Right

Put a tick (✔) on objects used for playing hockey.

Which Is Right

Put a tick (✔) on objects used for playing hockey.

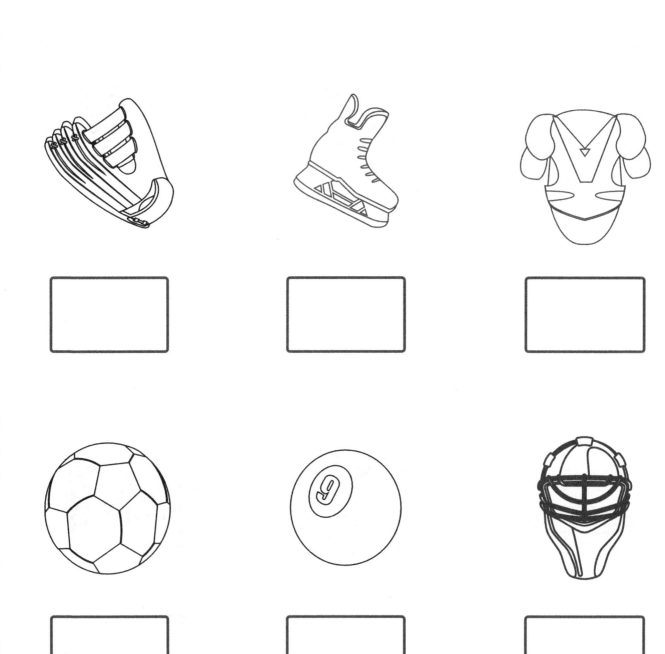

Which Is Right

Put a tick (✔) on objects used for playing hockey.

Which Is Right

Put a tick (✔) on objects used for playing hockey.

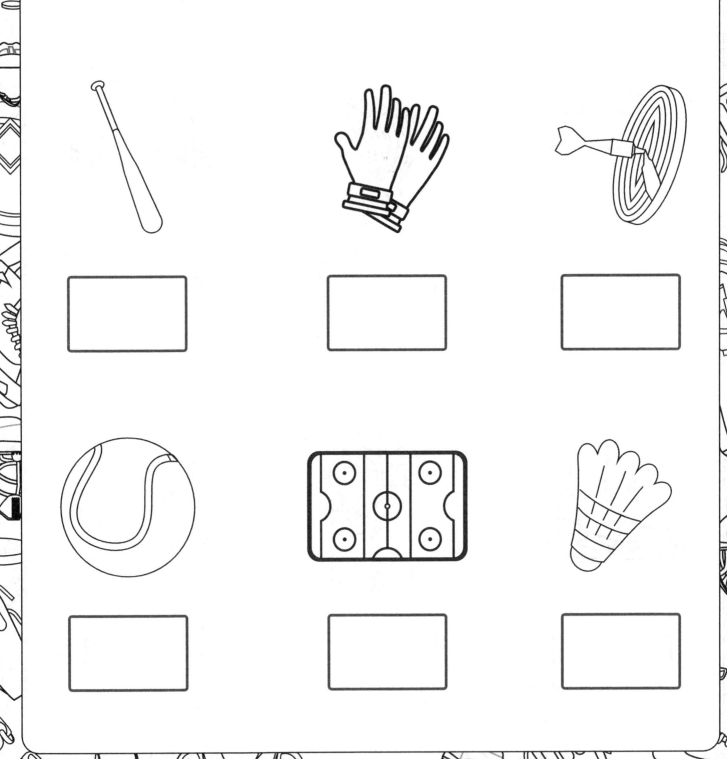

Which Is Right

Put a tick (✔) on objects used for playing hockey.

Find The Difference

Circle the different item in each group.

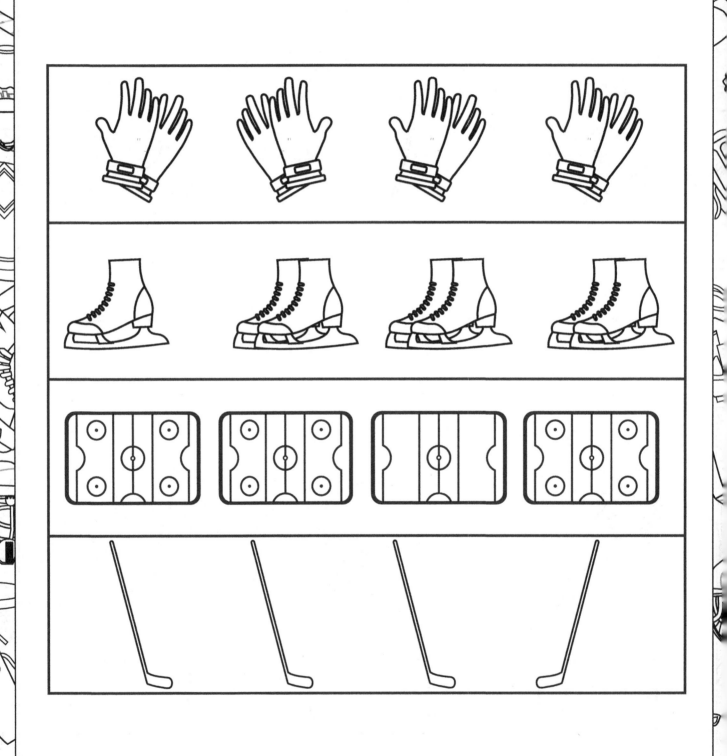

Find the Same Picture

Find and circle the same picture.

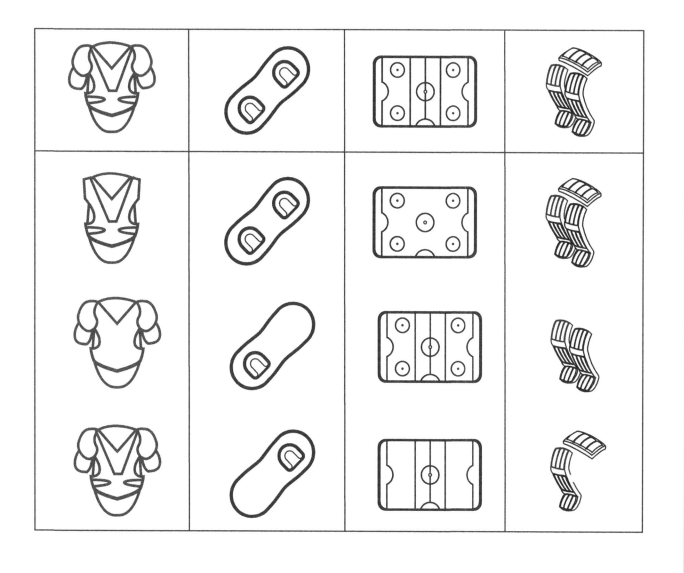

Find the Same Picture

Find and circle the same picture.

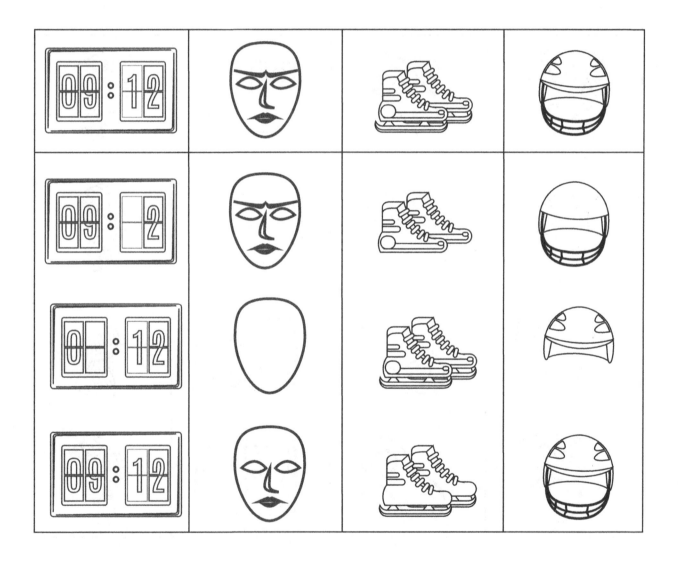

Find the Same Picture

Find and circle the same picture.

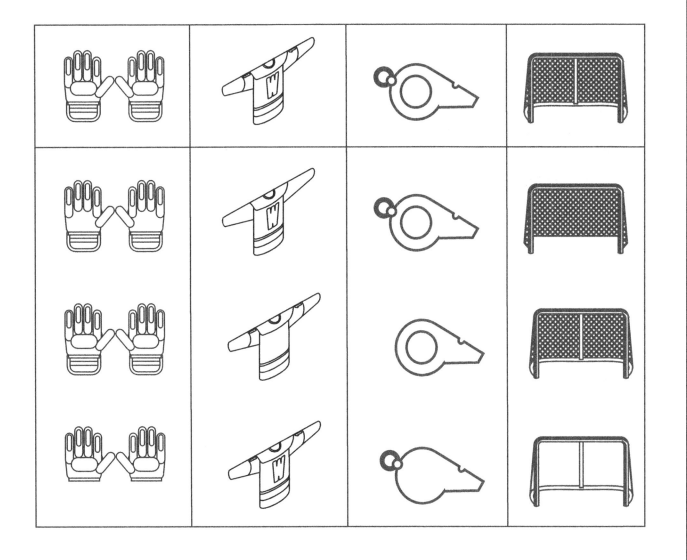

Find The Correct Shadow

Find and circle the correct shadow.

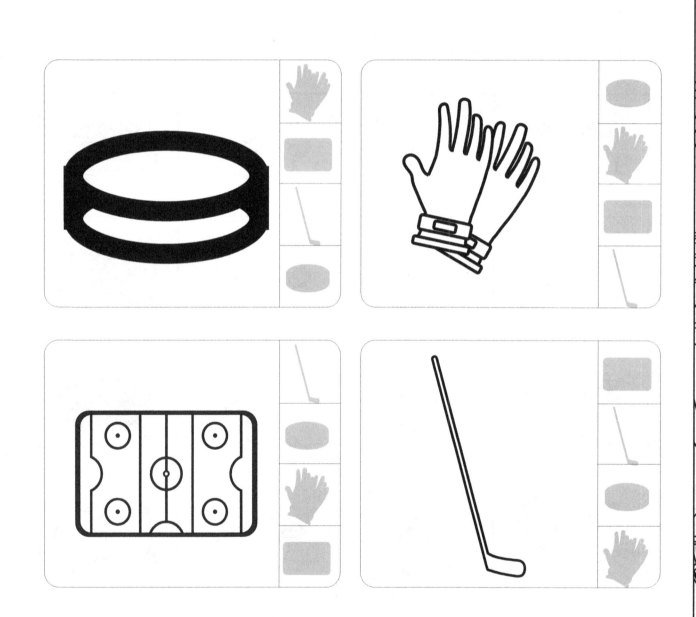

Find The Correct Shadow

Find and circle the correct shadow.

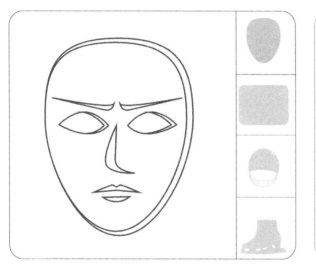

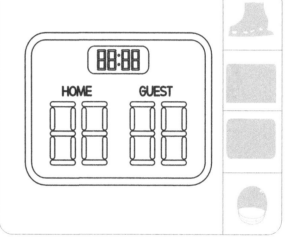

Find The Correct Shadow

Find and circle the correct shadow.

Find The Correct Shadow

Find and circle the correct shadow.

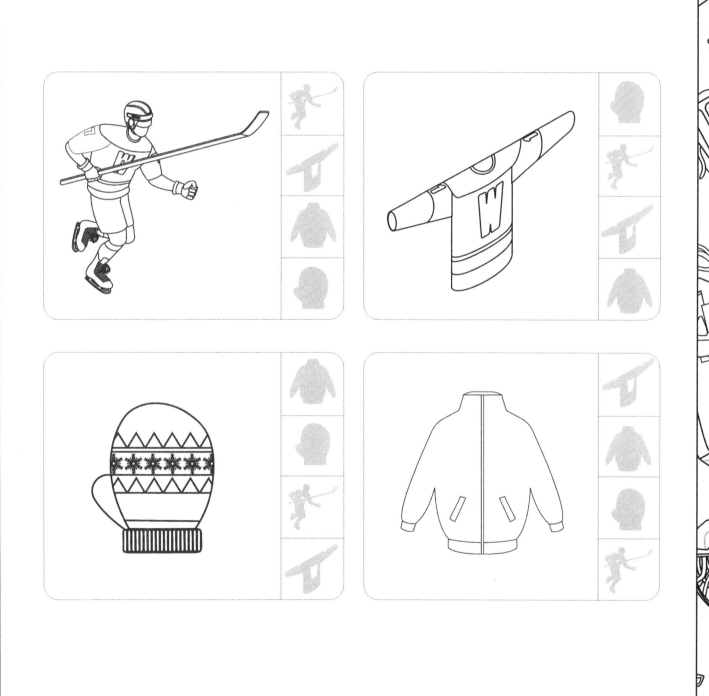

Find The Correct Shadow

Find and circle the correct shadow.

Find The Difference

Find and circle 7 differences between two pictures below.

Find The Difference

Find and circle 4 differences between two pictures below.

Find The Difference

Find and circle 4 differences between two pictures below.

Connect The Dots

Connect the dots below. Then color the picture.

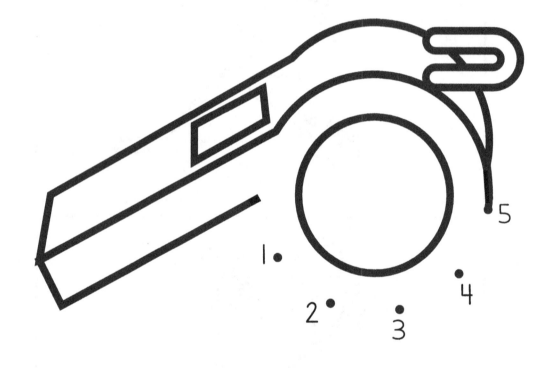

1.
2.
3.
4.
5.

Connect The Dots

Connect the dots below. Then color the picture.

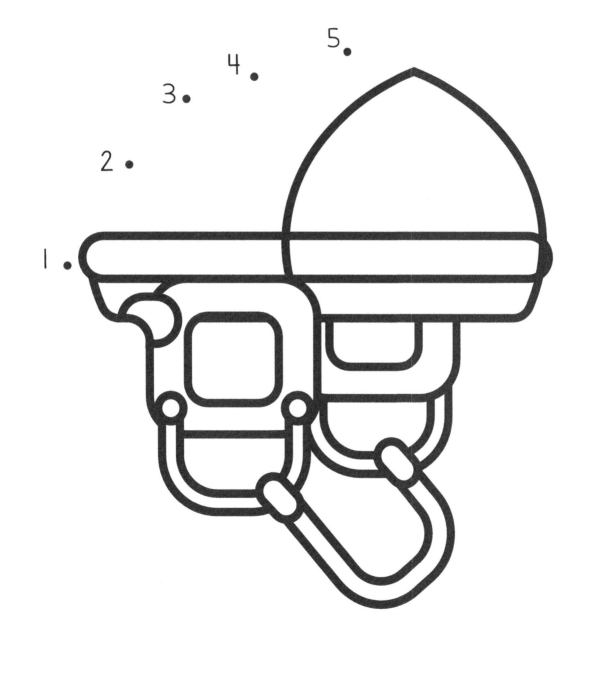

Connect The Dots

Connect the dots below. Then color the picture.

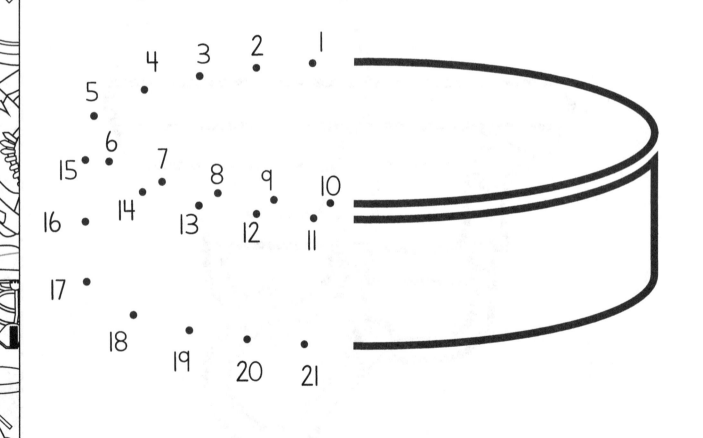

Copy the Picture

Draw and color the picture according
to the example image below.

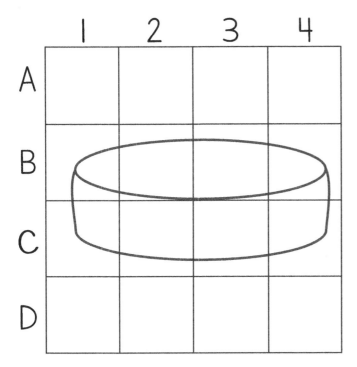

	1	2	3	4
A				
B				
C				
D				

Copy the Picture

Draw and color the picture according
to the example image below.

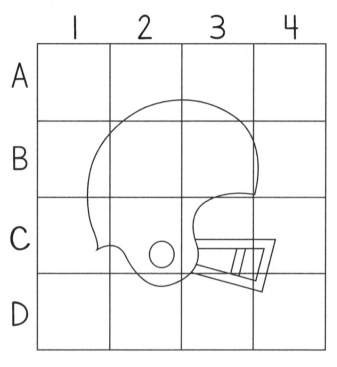

	1	2	3	4
A				
B				
C				
D				

Copy the Picture

Draw and color the picture according to the example image below.

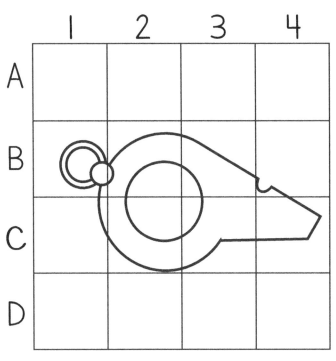

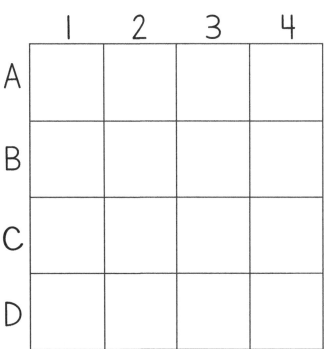

Copy the Picture

Draw and color the picture according
to the example image below.

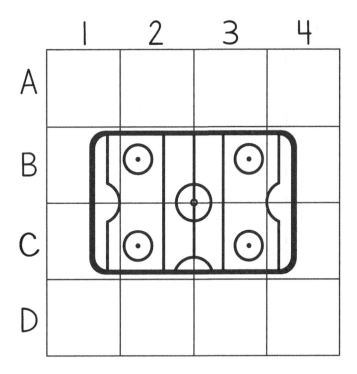

	1	2	3	4
A				
B				
C				
D				

Trace The Line

Trace the lines and color the picture.

Trace The Line

Trace the lines and color the picture.

Trace The Line

Trace the lines and color the picture.

Trace The Line

Trace the lines and color the picture.

Trace The Line

Trace the lines and color the picture.

Color By Numbers

Color the image below according to the specified colors.

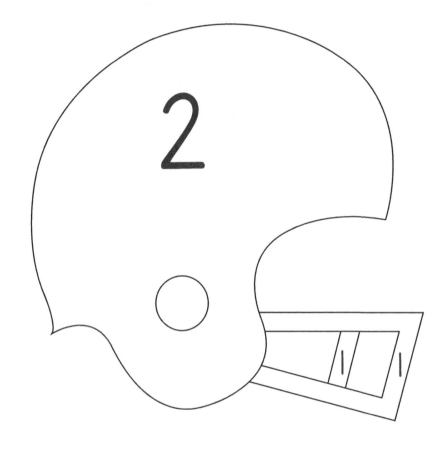

black   yellow

Color By Numbers

Color the image below according to the specified colors.

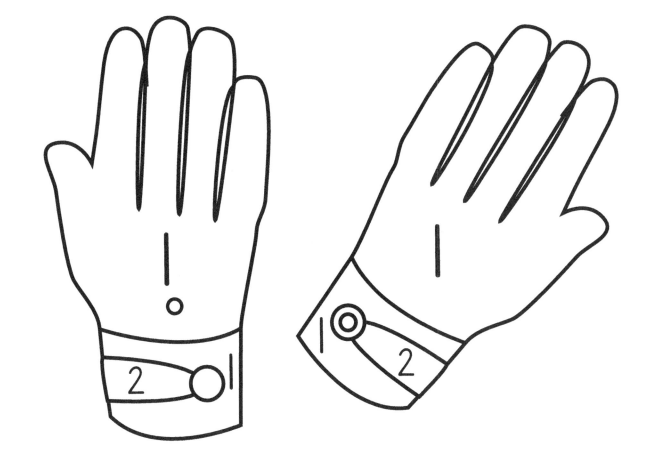

1 Red

2 Gray

Color By Numbers

Color the image below according to the specified colors.

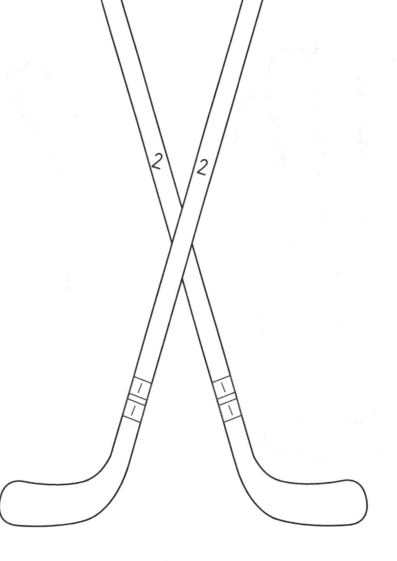

red 1

blue 2

Color The Picture

Color the picture of the puck below.

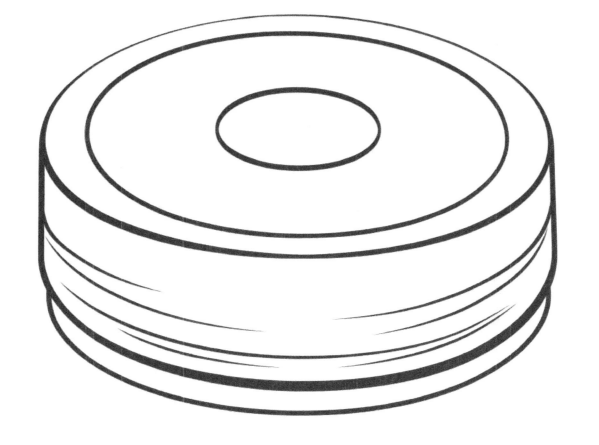

Color The Picture

Color the picture of the gloves below.

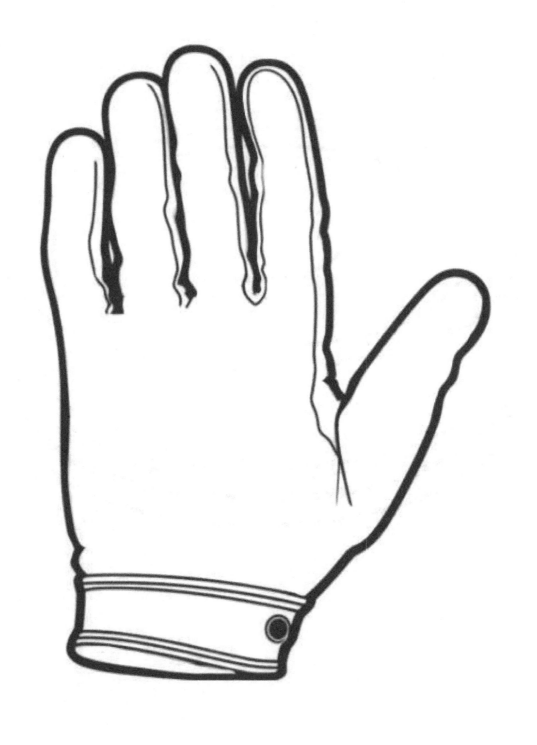

Color The Picture

Color the picture of the jersey below.

Color The Picture

Color the picture of the trophy below.

Color The Picture

Color the picture of the helmet below.

Color The Picture

Color the picture of the skate below.

Color The Picture

Color the picture of the person below.

Color The Picture

Color the picture of the person below.

Color The Picture

Color the picture of the person below.

Made in the USA
Monee, IL
01 July 2025

20320205R00052